FACE TO FACE WITH
LIONS

by Beverly and Dereck Joubert

NATIONAL
GEOGRAPHIC
WASHINGTON, D.C.

CONTENTS

Beverly and me in the bush, tracking lions.

FACE TO FACE: INTRODUCTION

Showing a perfect set of teeth, this lion's yawn sends a clear message: Any attacker will face powerful weapons of defence.

Most people don't really like getting up close and personal with lions. And that's a good thing, because lions are dangerous.

In many places in Africa, lions have attacked and killed people. But lions are not out to get you! They just want to mind their own business and stay out of trouble.

My wife Beverly and I have spent more than 25 years studying, filming and photographing lions – and trying to steer clear of their teeth.

HOW NOT TO GET EATEN BY A LION

- Lions are quite polite, and they expect the same from you. Never approach one directly from the front. You may be telling him you want to fight! Don't sneak up on him either.

- Wide eyes are a threat to a lion. Squint when you look at one. Never look at it directly.

- Don't run when you are near lions. They're cats, and cats love to chase. Back away slowly.

Sometimes, coming face to face with lions can be a little too exciting. One day, we accidentally came upon a pair of lions mating. Usually this is no problem if you give way, but the male was new in the area. We didn't know him, and he didn't know us. He charged from almost 200 metres away, the longest charge I have ever seen.

We live by an important rule out here. If a lion charges, we stand our ground. If we ran, it would turn into a cat-and-mouse game. And that's a game we couldn't win. So we faced down the angry lion. At 90 metres, he was showing no signs of giving up.

I said quietly to Beverly at my side, "Steady, just wait." She didn't break the silence. At 45 metres, after what seemed like an eternity, I could see the lion's bared yellow teeth and the amber red fire in his eyes. When he growled, I could smell his breath. "Steady," I said. Beverly was dead quiet. We were at the top of a three-metre-high riverbank, and I thought that he would stop at the bottom. Instead, he powered up, kicking and snarling at the sand.

Finally, to my surprise, I saw one of his hefty paws come up over the ridge. He was not more than a lion's leap away as he tried to haul himself over the edge – right at me.

Almost in slow motion, the sandy bank at my feet crumbled away. The lion fell back.

As he looked up at me, his eyes showed a flicker of disappointment. Then he turned away.

He slowly walked back to his female, who was growling in approval. No doubt, she was quite impressed.

It was only then that I discovered why Beverly had been so quiet. She wasn't there! Only her two shoes next to me marked the spot where she had stood.

Then I realised that she had probably done the right thing by slowly backing away. My brave showdown with the lion now seemed pretty daft. It is silly to test your strength against a lion.

🔺 *A male lion is easy to see across the plains. Squint your eyes to see his dark flag of a mane. Miles away, other males see this and know they had better keep their distance.*

MEET

*Frisky lion **cubs** are always attacking their mothers, leaping on their heads or ambushing their tails. Play is a way for young ones to learn the moves of a hunt, chase, and kill. But at first they may only hunt their poor mother's tattered ear!*

THE LION

*Mischief comes in small bundles. A male **cub** squeezes past his sister's legs to steal their mother's attention. Lions bond through touching, rubbing against each other and grooming.*

In all our years in Africa, we've been attacked by elephants, and a grumpy buffalo once bumped the car we were riding in. We've had close calls with snakes and scorpions. We've also had malaria and other diseases. But we've never had any major problems with the lions whom we have spent so much of our lives living with. Maybe it's because we know lions so well.

Where lions live

Lions live mainly in Africa. They **range** from the Skeleton Coast in Namibia, through the great Okavango Delta in Botswana, up into East Africa, and even into the forests of West Africa. A small number live in India. In each place they're different. For example, in the great plains of East Africa, you can see lions lolling around in the sun and hunting in the daylight. But in Botswana's Savute region, they usually hunt at night.

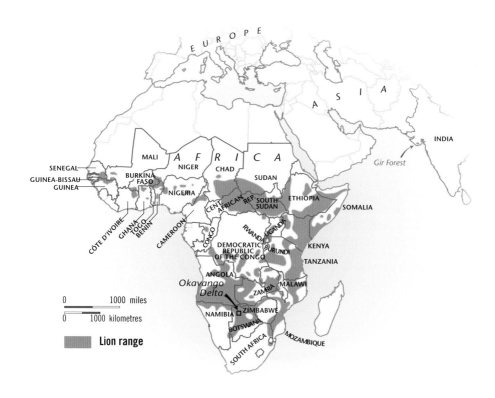

EUROPE

ASIA

AFRICA

INDIA

SENEGAL
GUINEA-BISSAU
GUINEA
MALI
NIGER
BURKINA FASO
NIGERIA
CHAD
SUDAN
Gir Forest
CÔTE D'IVOIRE
GHANA
TOGO
BENIN
CAMEROON
CONGO
CENTRAL AFRICAN REP.
SOUTH SUDAN
ETHIOPIA
SOMALIA
RWANDA UGANDA
DEMOCRATIC REPUBLIC OF THE CONGO
BURUNDI
KENYA
TANZANIA
ANGOLA
Okavango Delta
ZAMBIA
MALAWI
NAMIBIA
ZIMBABWE
BOTSWANA
MOZAMBIQUE
SOUTH AFRICA

0   1000 miles
0   1000 kilometres

Lion range

⬆ Lions once ranged across the entire African continent, but they are no longer found in the north and far south.

➡ The vast plains of the Okavango Delta make a magical backdrop for lions. More than 3000 lions live here, not far from our camp.

10

Powerful predators

Lions are known scientifically as *Panthera leo*. To understand them, you have to realise that they are **predatory carnivores**. That means they eat meat, and they have to kill to survive. But they are also picky eaters. In one area, they may hunt elephants for six weeks each year. In the Duba Plains, Botswana, where we live now, they hunt only buffalo and would never eat anything as

⬇ *Lions mate in a court-ship of flashing teeth and growling that can last up to a week. Cubs are born about three and a half months later.*

➡ *Mothers hide their cubs, moving them often so hyenas don't find them and kill them. When the cubs are a month or two old, their mum brings them into the **pride**.*

tough as elephant. They are adaptable, eating antelope in one area and living off seals on the beaches in another.

In the pride

Lion families are called prides. A pride of lions is usually made up of six to eight females, two males, and up to 24 cubs (or none at all). Each female can have four to six cubs at a time.

We love to watch lions with cubs. Sometimes you'll see the cubs running, leaping, biting an ear, attacking a tail. The cubs in a pride are usually born around the same time. They suckle the milk from any mother they come across at any time. After three or four months, I doubt whether the mothers even know which cubs are theirs.

By the age of a year, male and female cubs will join in all the activities of the pride. They even go along on hunts. In Duba, where we live, that means wading through water – although from the looks on their faces and their flattened-back ears, it seems like these "teenagers" are not that happy about getting their feet wet.

Lions, like all predators, have evolved to eat meat. It's the only way they can get enough energy to live. They tend to be messy eaters.

A LION'S LIFE

The kill. We are finding out that large predators are necessary for a healthy environment. Without them, herds of prey animals like zebras grow too large for the land to support. They eat all the plants, and the grassy plains can become a desert.

Being a lion must be wonderful, even though it is quite a short life. Lions can live about 15 years in the wild, but the oldest lion we ever filmed was 14 years old. One day while we were filming him, he walked toward us, fell over, and died.

Male lions leave their mother when they are about three years old, and the brothers wander around together as **nomads** for two years. This means they move from place to place, not settling in one area.

Lionesses hunt together, with each one doing the job she's best at. Older individuals stalk and separate one prey animal from the herd. Younger, faster ones give chase and leap on the prey.

Eventually, the brothers arrive in some far-off territory ready to challenge and fight for a new area to live in. Fights are usually brief – and dangerous. Lions are the heaviest cats in Africa. They are armed with long, strong teeth and razor-sharp claws, so even the winner can get badly injured. In fact, a lion would rather not fight. He prefers to roar and scare off his opponent if he can. So there is usually a lot of growling and spitting and hissing, and quite a bit of slapping.

Manes

A lion's shaggy mane of hair can form a scarf of protection around the throat. But females fight as well, so a mane can't have evolved solely as a defence. Scientists believe that a mane has many functions. A lion's long dark mane sends a clear signal to any intruders that this is his **territory** and that these females are claimed by a strong, healthy male. Females also seem to prefer males with darker, longer manes. These shaggy-haired males also seem to keep their prides together the longest. But there's a cost to being the handsomest male – these big manes can also cause **heat stress**.

⬆ Against massive opponents like a bull buffalo, lions have to cooperate. All the lionesses of this pride must be fit and healthy and working together to bring down prey of this size. It's a real struggle!

⬆ *It's not easy being a super predator. Hyenas sense that this lioness is injured. They gather to test her strength. At any sign of weakness, these clever and competitive predators will attack even the strongest cat in Africa.*

Even with his wild mane, the leader of a pride usually holds that rank for only two or three years. Then an outside challenger comes along and takes over.

Male lions that are beaten and thrown out of a pride often lose their manes. It's nature's way of helping them blend in and avoid attention from other lions.

Hunting

For a lion, no day is really complete without hunting. We have been filming some amazing buffalo hunts lately. The lions of Duba are huge, and they hunt in and out of water. Most cats hate the water, but these lions have adapted completely to the swampy conditions. One time, we saw lions attack a huge buffalo. They fought him for seven hours, thrashing in and out of the water, before the kill.

In Botswana, after the lions have worked hard for their meal and are just about to enjoy it, the hyenas arrive. Now, lions weigh almost twice as much as hyenas. But when hyenas get the scent of blood and have all their **clan** members by their side, they will swoop down and attack anyway. Hyena clans can have as few as ten or as many as 90 individuals. They can intimidate or bully the lions into sharing their kill. The hyenas can even send the lions running for the trees. But sometimes it's the other way around. Every once in a while, lions get to feast for free on kills that were brought down by hyenas.

HOW TO LIVE WITH <u>LIONS</u>

When you're staying on the African plains, or "in the bush", you are far away from the comforts of home.

- You live in a tent. A futon mattress makes a good bed.

- All your water comes from the river – for bathing, washing clothes and drinking. Be careful near the water though – sometimes crocodiles will attack!

- We've even used our jeep as a stove. We wrap food in aluminium foil and cook it on the hot engine. If the gravy spills, it smells good!

Every boss has a successful huntress behind him. Although male lions rule, females make 90 per cent of all lion kills.

THE FUTURE

*Lord and master of the **savanna**! Male lions dominate their prides. They sleep most of the day. They get to eat first at kills. They mate with all the females of the pride, and every cub obeys them.*

Lions have their own language, and if you read the signals, you can understand it, too. Humans don't always grasp the way things work in the lion kingdom, or they choose not to.

For example, when **safari** hunters shoot lions for recreation or sport, they usually select males with the biggest manes. But when they kill these big lions, they leave the pride with its smaller males. These lions with the smaller manes send a mixed signal across the savanna. It says, "I'm here, but I am not really in charge." As a result, more fights break out and more disruption in the prides occurs.

KEEP YOUR EYE ON THE LION

Want to visit your lion neighbours?

- Track them down by looking for a trail of bent grass.

- Look for a pride resting under some shady trees. Don't make noise or talk when you find them. Lions don't like to be disturbed!

When a lion is killed, naturally or by safari hunters, a new male comes in and takes over. Unfortunately, he immediately kills all the cubs. This allows the females to mate again, so the new male can raise his own cubs. As a result, each time a male lion is shot, up to 30 other lions might die.

We strongly believe that lions need to be in the wild. Today, however, many parks are just getting too small. So to save a lion, we have to save the land first. We may have to set aside more wildlife land. But that doesn't mean we have to kick all

⬆ *Tourism can bring much-needed money into Africa. If it's done right, with tourists taking photos from a safe distance, it can have little environmental impact.*

the people out of the way. Beverly and I live in the bush quite peacefully with lions around us every day. We may be an exception, of course, because we work with lions and have studied their behaviour.

Some African farmers raise cattle. Cattle and lions don't mix well, though. Cows are not native to Africa. They don't know how to defend themselves against big predators. To the lion, cows are easy prey! But if the cattle are kept in a safe place at night and are watched in the day, lions and cattle can coexist.

23

◀ When the sun goes down, the heat subsides. Everything relaxes just a bit. Lions go on the prowl again, roused from their daylight sleep. They are ready to patrol their territory and disappear into the darkness. Our job is to make sure they don't disappear forever.

Tourism is one thing that can help save the lions. Tourist lodges have been successful in Botswana. Travellers come to Africa on safari to see and photograph lions. They pay the lodge, and the local people get some money, too. The villagers build schools and clinics with money from tourism. They realise that lions can help them earn money.

Today there may be fewer than 25,000 wild lions left on Earth. There have never been as few as there are today. They are disappearing.

Lions can teach us how to behave in a gentler way toward the Earth. They don't run around slaughtering everything in their paths – even though they could. A little more compassion and friendliness will help save the world in the end.

HOW YOU CAN HELP

⬇ *Having a younger brother can be a pain in the neck! Especially if he has teeth like knives, claws like needles, and way too much energy.*

▬ Our "ecological footprint" describes how much space on Earth each of us needs. It includes the land we need to grow food, the carbon we release, the water we use, and our living space. See what you can do each day to reduce the impact that you have on the Earth. Recycle. Find out about global warming. Don't waste food or water. If we don't change, it won't just be the lions that run out of space!

▬ Think about how your actions affect the planet. If you throw a drink can out of the car window, who will pick it up? Will it land in the gutter and stay there, attracting rats and other creatures? Will it wash down into the sewer and make its way into a river or the sea? How long will it remain there?

▬ Saving lions starts at home. They need wild land. If we use up every piece of natural space, there will be more pressure on all wildlife.

▬ National Geographic's Big Cats Initiative is raising money to save lions and other big cats in 28 countries around the world. Maybe your parents would want to send them a donation, or maybe you could sometimes send them your pocket money. Go to nationalgeographic.org/projects/big-cats-initiative.

▬ Read as much as you can about lions. This knowledge could prepare you for encounters if you do go to Africa one day. It could even help you when dealing with any cat or wild animal.

IT'S YOUR TURN

Now that you know
a lot about lions,
would you like to observe
them yourself?

■ You can see lions in many zoos.
And maybe someday you can go to
Africa to see and photograph wild lions.

■ What interests you most about
lions? Cubs playing or learning to hunt?
Females raising their young? Males displaying their
handsome manes?

■ You can see many of these lion behaviours in a
zoo. You can watch lions at rest or cubs playing, or
hear a big male roar. Practise recognising individual
animals. Maybe one has a black-tipped tail, one
has a notched ear, or one is very small. Once you
know each of them, you will start to see how they
act within the group. It takes a lot of patience.
Don't make noises to disturb the lions. You want to
see them behaving naturally. You may have
to watch for a long time.

■ Take pictures and write captions about what
each photo shows, including where and when you
took it. A video camera can be fun to use too!

*▲ We called this female
cub Princess. When she
slipped and nearly fell
from a tree, she actually
looked embarrassed.*

Scientific Name
Panthera leo

Common Names
We sometimes refer to lions as big cats. In Africa, the lion has a few other names. In Botswana, we call them Tau. In Kenya, it is Simba. But when I see a huge lion, I usually just say, "Wow!"

⬆ *These playful lion cubs will grow up to be fierce predators, weighing around 190 kilograms.*

Features
Of the classic tawny-skinned cats of Africa, females weigh in around 122–136 kilograms and males weigh about 150–191 kilograms. In the swamps of Botswana's Okavango, they are about 15 percent larger because of their diet of buffalo. Females are less than 2.75 metres long. Males are up to 3 metres long.

Another feature of lions is their tremendous roar. Both male and female lions have a powerful roar that can be heard up to 8 kilometres away. It is not always one burst of sound. Sometimes it's a series: ROAR, uf, uf, uf, uf. If you're standing close by, it can actually hurt your head as the sound waves vibrate in your skull.

Diet
Lions eat just about anything, from mouse-like rodents called shrews to buffalo and elephants. But they prefer medium-sized prey like zebra and wildebeest. In Botswana, we have always found that they prefer buffalo.

Reproduction
Mating takes place over a full week. They don't feed at all during this time. Females carry the young for about 108 days on average. Litters consist of about three or

four cubs. Cubs are often born blind, or with milky, grey-blue eyes. They get black patches on the backs of their ears and tail tufts at five weeks. A five-week-old lion cub's paws are the size of those of a fully grown male leopard.

Status in the Wild

There are about 25,000 lions today in the wild. This is fewer than at any time in the history of lions. But lions are quite difficult to count accurately, so we may have more – or less! They range from the tip of Africa to the southern reaches of the Sahara and from the east to west coasts. There is even a small group of lions in the Gir Forest in India. This is a remnant population of a few hundred. They are all that's left from the days of old when lions spread right across Africa and Asia. The population in general has seriously declined.

Threats

"Canned" lion hunting and captive breeding have placed over 3000 lions behind bars in Africa. The canned hunting industry allows trophy hunters without the time, bravery, sense of what's right, or even sportsmanship to buy a lion in a cage, often hand-reared, and to shoot it. They then pretend that they have been on safari in Africa. This practice is now largely being banned.

Life span

In captivity, lions lead pampered lives. Hunting is just a distant dream.

They are much like domestic cats in this way. They can live into their 30s. But in the harsh wild world of Africa, where they have to hunt for food, lions live up to 15 years.

Home ranges

The lions we follow in Botswana have about 310 square kilometres of range for each pride. Males sometimes dominate two or even three female groups. They have extended ranges, but it depends on the habitat. In thick forests or swamps, lions have smaller territories and home ranges. In open plains their range expands.

A lion shakes pesky flies away.

GLOSSARY

Carnivore: An animal that eats mainly other animals.

Clan: A group of animals like hyenas that are related. They live and hunt together throughout their lives.

Cub: A young lion, from birth to 18 months.

Heat stress: This happens when a person or animal gets too hot and becomes ill as a result.

Nomadic: Wandering without a fixed territory.

Predator: An animal that preys on other animals as food.

Pride: A group of lions that live and hunt together.

Range: The area where a particular type of animal can be found.

Safari: Means "journey" in Swahili; in English, refers to an expedition into wildlife areas of Africa to photograph, observe, or conduct a hunt for trophies.

Savanna: A tropical grassland with scattered trees.

Territory: The area that one pride of lions lives in, hunts in and defends.

INDEX

RESEARCH & PHOTOGRAPHIC NOTES

So you want to photograph lions and big African wildlife? Imagine sitting in 53-degree-centigrade temperatures in the blazing sun for 12 hours straight, waiting for the kill. One time, the lions we'd been watching for days were all in position. We had so many cameras ready that the vehicle looked like a military gunship. Beverly's three Canon digital cameras with 600 mm, 400 mm, and wide-angle lenses were laid out on beanbags and tripods for stability. Each has a filter and lens hood to stop the sun flaring against the lens. I film with a big HD video camera and a massive lens on a tripod head mounted to the side of the vehicle. Suddenly the lions sprang, attacking the buffalo and isolating three bulls at the back of the herd. It was a fast-running chase. I was filming and Beverly was snapping away. The lioness came in like a bullet, gaining ground, getting closer and closer. She coiled up and launched herself into the air and then … nothing! The frame went black! My battery went dead at the exact instant of the attack! I grabbed a new battery, jammed it into place, and fired up the camera. I focused and started filming again … only to see that it was all over! Whenever this happens, Beverly and I give it some time and then laugh. If we didn't, we would hurl our cameras out of the car. Laughing at life and at ourselves seems to make it all okay. And it is okay – we'll be back again tomorrow!

Published by Collins
An imprint of HarperCollins*Publishers*
The News Building
1 London Bridge Street
London
SE1 9GF

Browse the complete Collins catalogue at
www.collins.co.uk

In association with National Geographic Partners, LLC

NATIONAL GEOGRAPHIC and the Yellow Border Design
are trademarks of the National Geographic Society, used
under license.

British English edition 2019
First published 2008 by National Geographic

ISBN 978-0-00-835806-8

10 9 8 7 6 5 4 3 2 1

British English Edition
Commissioning editor: Sarah Thomas
Content editor: Alexandra Wells
Educational reviewer: Catherine Baker
Design and typesetting: 2Hoots Publishing Services Ltd
Proof reader: Gaynor Spry
Production controller: Rachel Weaver
Printed and bound by: PNB PRINT, Latvia

This book is dedicated to lions.

Dear Lion, We thank you for all the opportunities, all the
laughter and fun you have brought to our lives, and
all the happiness and understanding we have been able to pass
on to the world. In the same way, we must apologise for all the
things we do to you as Man. Mostly we are ignorant twits, but
sometimes we get it right. The National Geographic Society
deserves special thanks for its support over 25 years of lion
work. I also wish to thank the President of Botswana, Fests
Mogae, the Vice President Lt. Gen. Ian Khama, the Department
of Wildlife and National Parks, its director, and staff; and the
people of Botswana, who have all adopted us as two weird lion
people. I was named Radetau, "father of the lions" in Setswana,
by the people of Botswana, but in so many ways we are Bana
ba Botswana, "children of Botswana", and very grateful of that.
Words struggle not to fall over themselves as poor and shabby
half-cousins in the shadow of great images like the photography
Beverly creates, and a book like this would be less colourful
(although cheaper) without her pictures. Besides that, she is my
soulmate, and a beautiful person inside and out.

If you would like to comment on any aspect of this book,
please contact us at the above address or online.
natgeokidsbooks.co.uk
collins.reference@harpercollins.co.uk

Since 1888, the National Geographic Society has funded more
than 12,000 research, exploration, and preservation projects
around the world. The Society receives funds from National
Geographic Partners, LLC, funded in part by your purchase.
A portion of the proceeds from this book supports this vital
work. To learn more, visit natgeo.com/info.

Beverly and Dereck Joubert have spent more than 25 years
in Africa studying, filming and photographing lions and other
creatures. This hardworking couple has created numerous
articles for *National Geographic* magazine, 20 films, and
six books. They have won countless awards, including four
Emmys and a Peabody. These National Geographic Explorers-
in-Residence have lived lives of adventure that most people
only dream of – struggling to survive in the bush, close to their
beloved big cats but far from modern conveniences and medical
care. They have dedicated their lives to the understanding and
conservation of Earth's magnificent places and creatures, and
they hope to share this love with children all over the world.